ANNA-MARIA'S MOCCASINS

By Nat Gabriel
Illustrated by Diana Magnuson

Celebration Press
Pearson Learning Group

CONTENTS

CHAPTER 1

WHO'S REALLY LUCKY?

MATT

Anna-Maria Gonzales is lucky. First, she's good at everything because she's super smart and even LIKES school. Second, her dad teaches math at the high school, so he probably taught her how to do long division before she could talk. She's a million miles ahead of the rest of the class, especially me.

Anna-Maria never gets nervous about tests or putting her work on the board. Her homework is always perfect, her handwriting is neat, and our teacher, Mr. James, likes her. For her, life must be a breeze.

I'm not saying my life is crummy or anything. Outside of school everything is terrific. My little brother's not so bad, and I think I've got the best mom and dad in the galaxy.

I'm also lucky because I'm good at playing soccer, which is the greatest game ever invented, if you ask me. My parents come to all my soccer games, and my dad likes to talk about all the plays with me afterward. I really have it good.

It's just that sometimes I wish I could snap my fingers and do better in school, or rub a magic lamp and wish for a brain like Albert Einstein's. Then maybe I'd understand math a little better. I'll tell you one thing. If I didn't have to do another long division problem for as long as I live, that wouldn't bother me one bit.

My dad works at night, and lately Mom has been too busy with my little brother to help

me much with my math homework. I try to do it on my own, but sometimes I just don't get it. All those numbers don't seem to make sense.

Besides schoolwork, there's only one other thing I'd change about my life. I'm afraid of something that I know I shouldn't be. If my friends ever found out, I'd be totally embarrassed. Only my parents know about it, and that's how I want to keep it—secret.

ANNA-MARIA

Matt Davis's life is perfect. He's so good-looking he could be a movie star. Girls bump into him in the hall just to get his attention! Of course, he wouldn't notice me if I bumped into him because I don't play soccer.

It seems as if almost everybody's on a soccer team—except me. One girl in my class, Miranda Kinney, is so talented that she plays on *two* teams. Matt always wants her to play on his team. Miranda's pretty, too. She's got a nose everybody thinks is cute, and she wrinkles it up when she smiles.

I don't think Matt likes me very much; he shakes his head and grumbles when Mr. James calls on me in math. He probably thinks I'm showing off, but I'm not.

My dad is a math teacher at the high school. He thinks math is about the most exciting thing in the world. Sometimes he gets this far-away look in his eyes, and Mom says, "Your father's left the planet again!"

I don't mind that he likes math. I like it,
too, but I wish I could kick a soccer ball as
well as Miranda does. Sometimes I try to
imagine what I'd do if Matt walked up and
said, "Hey, Anna-Maria, would you like me
to give you some soccer tips?" I think I'd
probably faint from happiness.

If he knew I even imagined such a thing, he
might laugh his head off. The Brain (that's
what everybody calls me) daydreams about
playing soccer with the most popular, perfect
boy in the class? As if that's going to happen!

CHAPTER 2

WINNING SOME AND LOSING SOME

MATT

Have you ever noticed that girls do things that don't make any sense? For instance, take Miranda Kinney. Almost every day she stops in the hall to ask me what time it is, even though she is wearing a watch, or asks if she can borrow a pencil when she has one already.

Miranda's a really good soccer player. She runs really fast, and she's a good passer. She's also a quick thinker, so she must realize that I know she's wearing a watch when she asks me the time. Not to mention this weird thing she does with her nose when she smiles. Maybe it's supposed to look cute or something, but I think it looks like she's smiling even though she smells something bad. I don't get it. Girls remind me a lot of long division—impossible to understand.

I like soccer because it makes perfect sense—all the time. It has rules, and if you break one, a whistle blows and you get a penalty. You know exactly what's going to happen. Simple.

Also, if you do something good, like make a great pass or kick a goal, then everybody claps and cheers, and the good feeling can last all day. When I get out on the field, it's easy. I know what I'm doing, so I'm completely comfortable. It's the only place in the world I feel that way.

Anna-Maria Gonzales must feel like that when she's in school. If I knew the right answers to every single question, the way she does, I wouldn't be afraid to raise my hand.

Mr. James is a cool teacher. He keeps fit and runs in marathons. I just wish he'd look at my answers and say, "Very good! I like the way you think!" That's what he always does with Anna-Maria.

What's amazing about her, besides that she's so brilliant, is that she doesn't ever brag about it. In fact, I think that sometimes she tries to hide it. A lot of times when Mr. James calls on her, her hand isn't even up. It doesn't make sense to me.

Mr. James sometimes watches us play soccer. Once he came over and told me he was impressed with a goal I made.

I felt great about him telling me that. Then he said, "I'd like to see more of that kind of enthusiasm in the classroom, Matt." It kind of wrecked the compliment, and I ended up feeling upset instead of proud.

"Who would like to volunteer to show us how they got the answer to the first homework problem?" Mr. James asked in math class this morning.

"Personally, I would rather take off my shoes and eat them for lunch," I thought to myself. I knew I didn't have the right answer. My stomach churned, and I looked down at my desk, hoping he wouldn't call on me.

ANNA-MARIA

I dread Monday mornings. For one thing, everybody talks about the soccer games and other sports they played over the weekend, and I feel totally left out. Miranda Kinney's father takes pictures at every game, and she's always showing them around.

She boasts, "Look, that's me kicking the goal that won the game!" It seems that she kicks the game-winning goal just about every weekend. You'd think no one else ever scored a point.

I asked my parents once not long ago if I could join a team, but my mom had already signed me up for piano lessons. My dad likes to spend "special time" with me on Saturdays, too. For my dad "special time" really means math time. He thinks math is fun, and he's always making up these clever brainteasers and math games. I love my dad, but math is *his* favorite thing in the world, not mine.

Mr. James asked for volunteers to show how they got the answer to one of the homework problems. I knew I could do it, but I hoped he'd call on somebody else.

I feel that the other kids are talking about me lots of times while I'm writing on the board. Mr. James is terrific, but he doesn't understand how I feel about going up to the board all the time, especially when I don't raise my hand.

"Anna-Maria, how about you?" Mr. James held the chalk out to me.

CHAPTER 3
DISASTER

MATT

Good, I was off the hook! It was lucky that Mr. James called on Anna-Maria, because the math homework had been about as clear as mud to me. I hadn't been able to finish many of the problems.

I watched Anna-Maria take the chalk and start writing. Her hands didn't shake while she was writing on the board the way mine always do.

I muttered, "The Brain does it again."

Mr. James shot me a look.

"Matt, do you have something to say to the class?" he asked.

I shook my head and looked down, just in case he was thinking about calling me up to the board. I sure didn't want to be up there next to Anna-Maria, where he could compare us.

I knew it was going to happen.

"Matt, would you like to try the next problem?" Mr. James asked.

"I, uh, I didn't really have a chance to finish this stuff last night, Mr. James. I, uh, had a soccer practice, you know, and I got home kind of late."

Mr. James looked at me. I felt my face getting hot and red.

"Even sports require a little math, you know, Matt," he said. "How do you think they figure out all those statistics?"

Mr. James smiled at me, but I'm not sure it's possible to feel any more embarrassed than I did when he said that to me. I must have turned red all the way down to my kneecaps. I could feel everyone looking at me, and I heard a couple of kids giggle behind their hands in the back of the classroom.

"I, uh, I didn't finish many of the problems, Mr. James," I said again, hoping he'd move on to someone else.

"Come on up to the board," Mr. James said. "Now I don't suppose you're in the mood to make fun of anyone else, are you, Matt?"

"Making fun?" I thought. "Was calling Anna-Maria the Brain making fun of her?"

Well, I have to admit that I did feel a little bit ashamed because she could work all the problems and I couldn't. I guess I felt a little jealous, too. I would have given anything right then to have a brain like hers inside my head.

I looked down at my paper. I was trying to see if there was any way I could figure out how to do the problem before going up to the board and getting laughed at again.

On her way back to her seat, Anna-Maria leaned over my chair and looked at the second problem on my paper.

"All you did wrong was that when you subtracted, you wrote two instead of the three," she said, "Here, I'll show you."

What happened next was totally my fault.

ANNA-MARIA

Matt Davis needed help. Maybe a small hint would be enough. I looked at his paper and spotted the mistake. Just as I was going to show him where it was, Matt stood up suddenly. Somehow I managed to fall over backward and hit my head on the desk behind me. It was totally my fault; I'm always so clumsy. One minute I was trying to help him with a math problem, and the next minute I was flat on the floor.

I wanted to disappear from the face of the earth I was so embarrassed. Girls are always doing things to get Matt's attention, but I end up falling down and making a big scene. I felt like crying.

"I hope I didn't hurt your, uh, your brain," Matt said, staring down at me.

I heard Miranda Kinney giggle.

"Don't worry, Matt. She's got brains enough to spare," Miranda said. "Even if she loses a few, she'll still have plenty left over to show us all up."

Is that what *everybody* thinks about me, that I'm a showoff? I don't ask to go up to the board; Mr. James asks me. Besides, I'm not the one who runs around with photographs of myself kicking game-winning goals *every* weekend, am I?

I was only trying to help Matt Davis, but I guess he didn't understand that, because right after Miranda said that mean thing, Matt laughed.

I couldn't help it; I started to cry.

MATT

Just as I was getting up to go to the board, I felt myself bump into someone. I turned around and Anna-Maria was falling backward. When I saw Anna-Maria's head hit a desk, I got really nervous because I thought she might be hurt. When I'm nervous I laugh, so even though Miranda Kinney made fun of Anna-Maria, I laughed. I didn't think it was funny; honest I didn't. I just laughed because I was nervous. A lot of the other kids laughed, too, at first.

Then Anna-Maria started to cry, which was just awful. I looked at Miranda to see if she was going to do anything, but all she did was smile and wrinkle her nose. She is so bizarre!

Mr. James jumped up and ran over to see if Anna-Maria was okay. Then I knew I was in big trouble. I was sure he wouldn't believe me when I told him it was an accident.

Anna-Maria told Mr. James she wasn't really hurt. Then she said in a low voice, "You have no idea how hard it is to be me."

I was so surprised that I didn't know what to say. Hard to be her? Was she kidding? What's hard about being totally perfect? So far I'd made a fool out of myself twice, first by not knowing the right answer to the math problem and then by knocking her over. I didn't know what to say, so I didn't say anything at all.

Mr. James looked at me and shook his head. I could tell he thought I should do something, but I didn't know what.

If Mr. James hadn't heard what Anna-Maria said to me, he might have just decided to punish me by sending me down to the principal's office. After I got back, I would have told everybody that it was an accident. Then I would have apologized to Anna-Maria for laughing, and the whole thing would have ended right there. That's not what happened though—not by a long shot.

"Are you going to send me to the principal's office?" I asked.

"Sending you downstairs to wait until Ms. Ramos can see you when we still have math time left seems more like a reward than a punishment, Matt," Mr. James said. "Instead, I want you to get back to work. Then both you and Anna-Maria remain after class. I want to talk to you two about something." Then he went back to his desk.

"What do you think he wants to talk to us about?" I asked Anna-Maria. I held out my hand to help her up.

Anna-Maria ignored me and got up by herself. I felt embarrassed and awkward. I wanted to tell her how sorry I was about her hitting her head; I wanted to tell her that I didn't laugh because I thought it was funny; I wanted to tell her that I hadn't thought being called the Brain would really hurt her feelings so much. I wanted to tell her all those things, but as usual, I couldn't seem to find the right words.

CHAPTER 4
WALKING IN SOMEBODY ELSE'S SHOES

ANNA-MARIA

I wanted to tell Matt I was sorry that I'd butted in on his homework. Did he know how embarrassed I was that I'd fallen down like that, I wondered. I didn't want Mr. James to blame him, but I was so flustered I just couldn't say anything.

Matt held out his hand to help me get up, but I wanted him to see that I wasn't some weakling who couldn't even get up by herself.

"What do you think Mr. James wants to talk to us about?" he asked me.

I didn't care what Mr. James was going to say. I just wanted this whole thing to be over and forgotten—the sooner the better.

After school Matt and I stayed until all the other kids had left. Miranda Kinney took an

extra long time getting her backpack ready. I could tell she was trying to stick around long enough to find out what was happening. Mr. James knew what she was doing, though, and asked her to hurry up. After she left, he closed the door.

"Okay. I spoke to your parents today, Matt, and yours, too, Anna-Maria," he began. "I wanted to see if they would go along with a plan I've come up with."

"What kind of a plan?" I asked.

Mr. James smiled and cleared his throat.

MATT

I've always liked Mr. James, even though he teases me sometimes. However, what he said that day after school made me wonder if he'd gone crazy.

"Matt, I want you to go to Anna-Maria's house on Saturday morning and walk a mile in her moccasins."

"What?" I said.

"I don't have any moccasins, Mr. James," said Anna-Maria with a perplexed look on her face, "and even if I did, I don't think they'd fit him."

Mr. James laughed. "Let me explain. There's an expression that goes like this: 'You never really know a man until you've walked a mile in his moccasins.' Do you understand what that means?"

I looked at Anna-Maria. She nodded as she glanced over at me. Of course she understood. I, on the other hand, had no idea what he was talking about.

ANNA-MARIA

Did Mr. James say what I thought he said? Did he really expect Matt Davis to come to my house? Was he crazy? Why in the world would Matt agree to do that? He probably had a soccer game or at least a practice on Saturday. He'd hate giving that up just to figure out how it feels to be me!

"Can't I just tell Matt a couple of things about how it feels to be me, so he doesn't have to miss his soccer game, Mr. James?" I asked.

Matt had a strange look on his face.

"I already checked with Mr. Davis. There's no game or practice this Saturday. I really want you to give this plan a try. I have a feeling you'll both learn something."

"I'm sorry I knocked her over, Mr. James," said Matt. "Honestly, I really am, but can't you find a different kind of punishment? Something that's not so weird?"

"It's not a punishment, Matt. It's more like a learning experiment. Anna-Maria, I got the idea from what you said after you hit your head," said Mr. James. "I think you're right. Matt probably doesn't know how it feels to be you."

"No kidding," I thought. "For one thing, he's got better things to do than spend his weekends sitting around doing math problems with his father."

"So, Matt, I'd like you to be at Anna-Maria's house at nine o'clock sharp on Saturday morning," Mr. James continued. "I'll look forward to hearing all about it first thing on Monday."

MATT

Why was I going to Anna-Maria Gonzales's house on Saturday morning? Why would she want me to? And what did any of it have to do with her moccasins, which she said she doesn't even have?

I could tell by the look on Mr. James's face that this was a done deal, though, and that there was no use arguing. So I said the only thing I could at that point to Anna-Maria.

"Okay, see you on Saturday."

Anna-Maria shrugged her shoulders. "Yeah," she said.

We got our backpacks and left.

"Good luck!" Mr. James called after us.

I told only one friend at school about Saturday, but by the end of the week, Miranda Kinney had found out somehow.

"Gee, Matt, I wish you were coming over to my house," she said, wrinkling up that crinkly nose of hers. "I bet we'd have more fun than you will hanging around with the Brain."

I looked around and was glad to see that Anna-Maria was too far away to hear Miranda. I'd been thinking about why people thought that nickname was mean. I still wasn't completely sure, but just hearing it made me nervous. So, of course, I laughed, even though nothing that Miranda said was the least bit funny.

ANNA-MARIA

"Well, I'm glad to see somebody thinks this is funny," I thought. Matt and Miranda were looking over at me and laughing during lunch on Friday.

"You should see her father and his silly math games," he'd fill her in on Monday.

"Oh, Matt. How could you stand to spend a whole day with that boring Anna-Maria?" she'd say as she flipped her hair over her shoulder and smiled that cute smile at him.

Thinking about it made me feel sick. Why was Mr. James making us do this?

CHAPTER 5
SECRETS REVEALED

MATT

When Anna-Maria opened her front door at nine o'clock on Saturday, the first thing I saw was her dog. Okay, here's my big secret. I'm actually afraid of dogs. Isn't that ridiculous? Any kind of dog, big or little, makes me want to jump out of my skin.

"This is Geometry," she said, extending the dog's paw for me to shake.

The dog had a mathematical name, which was perfect, of course, for Anna-Maria's pet— a combination of my two least favorite things. I'd never seen such a tall dog in my life.

"Uh, I'd better not touch him. I'm allergic," I said, hoping she wouldn't be able to tell it wasn't true.

"Oh," she gave me a suspicious look.

I was sure she could see right through me.

ANNA-MARIA

I could tell Matt thought I was weird. Why did I have to go and do something silly like asking him to shake hands with my dog? Miranda Kinney would never do something uncool like that. I couldn't help it; I was nervous. Matt Davis was standing on my porch.

He said he was allergic to dogs. He didn't get a rash or start sneezing or anything, but I could tell he was uncomfortable.

"Is that Matt?" Dad called from inside.

"Come on in," I said. "I'll put Geometry in the kitchen so he won't bother you."

After putting Geo in the kitchen, I came back out to find Matt and my dad shaking hands. My dad does things like shake hands with kids even though I've asked him not to.

"How about we break the ice with some math games?" my father said.

I rolled my eyes. I wished Dad wouldn't do that, just this once!

"Here we go," I thought. "All aboard the Anna-Maria-Gonzales-is-a-totally-boring-math-nerd train."

I looked over at Matt, and he looked even more uncomfortable than when Mr. James calls him up to the board to show his math homework.

"Dad, do we have to?" I asked. "Matt doesn't really like math very much, you know. He's more into soccer."

MATT

The nightmare had begun.

"Matt doesn't really like math very much," Anna-Maria told her father. Translation: "Dad, Matt Davis is as dumb as a post. All he can do is kick a ball around the soccer field. Don't waste your time with him."

"Oh, come on. It'll be fun," Mr. Gonzales said. He pulled out a box of match sticks and dumped them on the table.

I heard the dog scratching and barking just outside the door, and I felt the hair on the back of my neck prickle. "Please let that door be shut tight," I thought.

For the next 45 minutes we played math games. I've never thought of math as a game, but the way Mr. Gonzales did it—and I can't believe I'm saying this—it was actually fun. Math was fun.

The other thing I can't believe is that I was pretty good at it. Somehow, seeing all those match sticks being divided up into little piles made everything seem clearer to me. For the first time I actually got long division!

"I thought you said you weren't into math," Mr. Gonzales said at one point. "You're a natural and very bright. All you lack is confidence."

Somehow I felt as proud as if I'd just kicked a game-winning goal. I looked at Anna-Maria and smiled.

ANNA-MARIA

Matt did just fine with my father's math games. Dad even called him a "natural," which made Matt look at me and smile. I felt as if I was going to rise up into the air like a balloon. Then it hit me. He was amused thinking about how much fun it was going to be to tell Miranda about what a boring time he'd had at my house.

Geo had been barking at the door for a while. Now he had managed to push it open and come in. I was about to put him back in the kitchen, but then I thought, "Why should I? Matt doesn't care how I feel. Why should I care about his dumb dog allergy?"

MATT

Anna-Maria stopped smiling. In fact, she looked angry. What did I do wrong?

Then all of a sudden I saw him. The dog! Not only was he free, he was heading straight for me. I know you're not supposed to let a dog know you're scared of him, but I was so freaked out that I was shaking all over. All I could think was, "If Anna-Maria tells the kids at school about this, my reputation is ruined."

Anna-Maria and her father both stared at me.

"What in the world?" Mr. Gonzales asked. "You're not afraid of Geometry, are you?"

That's when Mrs. Gonzales came in with some juice and a plate of cookies.

"How's it going?" she asked cheerfully, not realizing right away that something was wrong.

ANNA-MARIA

Matt Davis was looking at Geo and shaking.

"What on earth is going on?" my mother asked.

"He's allergic," I said, trying to keep him from being embarrassed. I grabbed Geo and shoved him into the kitchen.

My mother tried to calm Matt. "I don't see any hives, and your breathing seems okay," she said.

"Matt, do you think maybe you're a little afraid of the dog?" my father asked gently.

Matt turned red and looked as if he was going to die of embarrassment.

CHAPTER 6

MAKING AMENDS

MATT

I was mortified when Mr. Gonzales asked if I was afraid of the dog. Then I couldn't believe my ears. Anna-Maria said, "No, Dad, he really is allergic. Everybody knows it."

"Well, we'll have to get Geo out of here before he causes Matt any more discomfort," Mr. Gonzales said. Then both he and Mrs. Gonzales went out of the room. I could tell they weren't convinced, but it made me feel better anyway.

"You ARE afraid of him, aren't you?" Anna-Maria asked.

I nodded. "Go ahead and tell everybody," I said. "It will be the perfect way to get back at me for knocking you over."

"You didn't knock me over. I lost my balance, and I fell over."

"Then why were you so mad at me afterwards?" I asked.

ANNA-MARIA

"I wasn't mad," I said. "I was embarrassed because you and Miranda were laughing at me."

"I was just nervous. I laugh when I'm nervous," Matt explained. Then he laughed. "See?"

I laughed, too.

"Do you think the Brain is an insulting nickname?" Matt asked me all of a sudden.

"That all depends," I said, "on who's saying it and how they mean it."

"When I say it, it's not supposed to be insulting," Matt said. I felt that rising balloon sensation again.

MATT

"Are you going to tell everybody at school about the dog thing?" I asked Anna-Maria.

"Not if you don't want me to," she said.

"Really?"

"Are you going to tell them about playing math games with my dad?" she asked.

"Don't you want me to?" I asked her.

"Not really."

"Okay," I said, "I won't tell then."

"Not even Miranda?"

"Why would I tell Miranda anything?" I asked. "She's always doing something goofy like asking me the time when she's already wearing a watch," I said. "Didn't you ever notice that?"

"She just wants you to pay attention to her," Anna-Maria explained. "I thought you liked her."

"Not really. She does that weird thing with her nose, too. You know—" I wrinkled my nose up, and Anna-Maria laughed.

"You mean you don't think that's cute?" she asked.

"No. She's a good soccer player, though," I answered.

"I wish I were good at soccer," Anna-Maria said wistfully.

"Have you ever tried?" I asked.

"A little bit, but I think I'm awful at it."

"Maybe I could give you some tips to help you get better," I said.

ANNA-MARIA

Was I dreaming or had Matt Davis just offered to teach me how to play soccer better? He doesn't know just how much help I need.

"I should warn you. I think I might be hopeless," I said.

"That's what I thought about math, too, but your dad said I'm a natural. Do you think he really meant that?"

"Yeah, I do," I laughed. My dad doesn't give compliments unless they're well deserved.

"Your dad is pretty cool. Do you think, maybe—oh never mind," Matt said.

"No, what? Do I think maybe what?" I asked.

"Do you think maybe I could come over another Saturday and do more of those math games with you?" Matt asked.

"That all depends." I could feel a big smile on my face. "Do you think you could teach me how to dribble better or how to do a header?"

"No problem," Matt said. "Somebody as smart as you will probably learn fast. Let's start with some footwork."

"Are you sure we shouldn't work on balance first? You know, sometimes I fall over," I joked.

"Most people do when somebody like me bumps into them."

Matt laughed and kicked the soccer ball toward me.

MATT

At the start of math class on Monday morning, Mr. James asked for volunteers to solve one of the homework problems on the board. I raised my hand. I knew I could do it right.

"Well, well, Matt Davis! Come on up and show us what you've got," he said, sounding a little surprised.

I solved the problem just the way Mr. Gonzales had shown me on Saturday. My hand didn't shake, and I wasn't nervous. I understood what I was doing. It felt really great.

"Nice work!" Mr. James said. "Very nice work indeed, Matt."

On the way back to my seat, I looked at Anna-Maria, and we both smiled.

ANNA-MARIA

After lunch I felt pretty nervous. Matt called across the soccer field to me.

"Come on, Gonzales. You're on my team."

Miranda Kinney's mouth fell open so wide I could have walked inside it. When the game was almost over, Mr. James came out to watch us play.

"Okay, remember what I showed you," Matt called to me as he dribbled the ball with his feet. He was flying along fast towards the goal.

Matt made it look like he was going to kick the ball into the goal, but instead at the last minute, he kicked it up high in the air. I ran toward it, remembering exactly what he taught me. I closed my eyes and smacked it with my head. It shot straight into the net.

Mr. James cheered. Matt and I whooped. Miranda Kinney, who was playing on the other team, did not look the least bit happy.

"They don't call you the Brain for nothing," Matt called. "You sure know how to use your head!"

Somehow I didn't mind my old nickname anymore. Nope, not one little bit.